Angelo Morgan-Somers

Do Bitcoin

The future of money.
And what you need to know.

Book Co

Published by
The Do Book Company 2022
Works in Progress Publishing Ltd
thedobook.co

The right of Angelo Morgan-Somers
to be identified as author of this
work has been asserted by him in
accordance with the Copyright,
Designs and Patents Act 1988

A CIP catalogue record for this book
is available from the British Library

ISBN 978-1-914168-10-9

10 9 8 7 6 5 4 3 2 1

To find out more about our company,
books and authors, please visit
thedobook.co or follow us **@dobookco**

5 per cent of our proceeds from the sale
of this book is given to The DO Lectures
to help it achieve its aim of making
positive change: **thedolectures.com**

Cover designed by James Victore
Book designed and set by Ratiotype

Printed and bound by OZGraf Print
on Munken, an FSC-certified paper

MIX
Paper from
responsible sources
FSC® C163799

Disclaimer
The information in this book has been
compiled by way of general guidance
in relation to the specific subject
addressed, but is not a substitute and
not to be relied on for financial advice.
Please consult your financial advisor
before investing in cryptocurrency.
So far as the author is aware the
information given is correct and up to
date as at 2022. Laws and regulations
change and the reader should obtain
up to date professional advice on
any such issues. The author and
publishers disclaim, as far as the law
allows, any liability arising directly or
indirectly from the use, or misuse, of
the information contained in this book.

Contents

Prologue

Books are great. They cause us to organise all our ideas and learnings into words with care and consideration. They take a great deal of thought and effort to put together, so the author (almost) always cares deeply about the topic they write about. I am one such author.

Firstly, I would like to introduce myself, explain how I came across Bitcoin and show you why I believe it's a topic more than worth writing a book about. So, I guess I'll start with hello! My name is Angelo Morgan-Somers. I'm a young Bitcoin investor and consultant from a small village in Southwest Wales, United Kingdom. I left the education system when I was 12 years old following a severe parkour accident. The shortness of life became all too obvious when the doctors told me every physical movement was a roll of the metaphorical dice of mortality. Therefore, once I healed, I set out to educate myself online about subjects I believed to be necessary, rather than spending my finite years slowly half-learning a plethora of mandatory curriculum subjects in which I had no interest and to which I attached no sense of importance.

Discovering money

One year later, after realising money is pretty important —
who would've thought? — I came across a new project
called Ethereum ... and so it began. The world of so-called
'cryptocurrencies', and digital money such as Bitcoin,
presented itself to me.

The crypto community often talks about 'going down
the rabbit hole'; to be honest, I have yet to find a better
metaphor to describe what learning about crypto feels
like, other than kissing an oncoming train, maybe. This is
because crypto is a subject that combines a lot of topics,
including computer science, programming, economics,
history and game theory, to name a few. Combine that with
the lack of quality educational materials, and suddenly
crypto attains a mythos of complexity that has learners up
to their necks in books and YouTube videos. Crypto doesn't
need to be that complicated. This 'going down the rabbit
hole' journey is often more difficult because of unnecessary
jargon, information overload and scatter-gun teaching.

Discovering Bitcoin

Once I got past the jargon, I adopted a first-principles
approach to learning. I realised that Bitcoin is technology
and, like all technologies, it must have been created to
solve a problem. So, I asked myself: 'To what problem is
Bitcoin a solution?' The answer to this question birthed
an 'Aha!' moment for me. Bitcoin was no longer just weird
internet money. I realised that it has enormous potential to
change the world for the better. The reason that I believe
this to be true will become increasingly apparent as you
continue to read this book. I hope I can show you that

'changing the world' in the 21st century might not look like gunpowder and revolution, but rather a few lines of immutable code, an idea, and some crazy internet nerds willing to dedicate their lives to the improvement of the two fundamental entities upon which the direction of human progress is determined: energy and money.

Introduction

Picture something you understand. I don't mean something you just 'sort of understand'; I mean something you know you understand. It could be how to send an email, how to tie your shoes, a subject in your field of expertise or even how to drive a car ... go ahead, picture it. Now let me ask you a question: does it seem very confusing? If you answered yes, then maybe reconsider your understanding of the subject; however, if you responded no, welcome to the club.

I'm sure many things you understand are complex. However, I doubt they feel *confusing*. Confusion is just the subjective counterpart of complexity. Things that we genuinely understand are almost always things that we once overestimated the complexity of. Everybody has had the 'penny drop' moment with something difficult in their lives, where somebody delivers a proper explanation only for the perceived complexity of the subject to vanish. The unclear understanding you had suddenly seems to sink into place. A deeper understanding emerges, and you follow through with an 'It's so obvious! How could I have missed that?' You're left with a cohesive mental model that accommodates all the facts and variables that just wouldn't play nice with each other before. For this reason, I don't believe it would be too far-out a statement to say:

Nothing is complicated; some things are just harder to explain.

So that is the goal of this book: to explain Bitcoin properly, in a way that doesn't have you pulling your hair out, so you can reach a decent level of understanding about the cryptocurrency industry and all its historical, cultural and technological implications.

Memory vs. models

Memorising '5 × 5 = 25' is easy, but truly understanding that expression requires a first-principles understanding of what numbers are, what multiplication is and what it means for one thing to be equal to another. This context provides the space for deep understanding to arise. For more than just mathematics, it is true that the requirement of context precedes understanding in the learning process. For instance, while I was learning about Bitcoin in 2016, the learning materials I used would skip over this crucial part: context. They flooded me with internet-money jargon such as 'miners' and 'distributed consensus mechanism', and I was still entirely unaware of *why* Bitcoin exists.

The importance of context

As I continued learning, I realised that money is a technology
with an array of limitations — of which the human species
has been attempting to break free for thousands of years.
Bitcoin is our latest attempt. Once I learned what money
is and the multifaceted problem it endeavours to solve,
I understood the Bitcoin solution ... and I thought it was
a terrible idea. That was until I learned about the system
of exchanging value that we so generously call 'money'
today. Today's money, in its current form of enforced paper
acceptance, which my 13-year-old self always assumed had
existed for all time and was delivered by the gods, turned
out to have inhabited earth for less time than my parents.
Additionally, compared to history's previous forms of money,
it read like a George Orwell novel: dystopian. Not only
this, but those forms of money littered throughout history
solved just a tiny portion of the problems that have been
solved by Bitcoin; I thought Bitcoin sucked because my
learning lacked contextual contrast.

Let's get you up to date

This book will first explain the problem that money
attempts to solve, to provide context on why Bitcoin exists,
before explaining the solution: blockchain. Once I have
summarised how the Bitcoin blockchain works, you
will have a general sense of how all blockchains work.
However, just as understanding how HTTP (Hypertext
Transfer Protocol) works isn't necessary to understand
why the internet matters, understanding exactly how
every blockchain works isn't necessary to understand
why blockchain matters (and what you should do about it).

My goal is that by the end of this book, you will feel comfortable in your understanding of why Bitcoin and the cryptocurrency industry are drawing so much attention and what you should do to get involved so that 20 years from now, you can sit with a smile on your face and say, 'I was an early adopter of Bitcoin!' with pride.

Part one:
**What's wrong
with our money?**

1
What is money?

When asked 'What is money?' people often fail to give an accurate response. A standard answer goes like this: 'We use it to pay for things.' While a true statement, this doesn't answer the question.

The question asks *what* money is, and that answer explains one of the many uses of money. It's a correct answer to the wrong question; it'd be like asking 'What is a computer?' and getting the response 'We use it to google things.' It's a sneaky way to avoid answering a question that you aren't entirely sure of. While we certainly use *some types* of computers to google things, computers are electronic-circuit devices for data storage and calculation. Sure, it's a bit of a mouthful, but it's still a much more accurate response to the question. Your car has a computer inside it, but I doubt you have ever used it to google something.

Therefore, definitions are very important if you want to understand the greater purpose something serves to society. If you ask yourself 'What is money?' and attempt to answer it without explaining what it's used for, or just naming one of the various types of money such as United States dollars or British pounds, you will find it's not so straightforward as it seems. To use the computer analogy again, it would be like answering 'A computer is an iPhone,' when in fact it isn't. An iPhone is a computer, but a computer is not an iPhone; the British pound is money, but money is not the British pound.

All right, enough questions; time for some answers. This is likely one of the book's most important chapters, so bear with me while I set up this metaphor.

Energy

The simplest definition for energy is the capacity or ability to do work (affect things), such as moving an object of a given mass. If you read this entire book in one sitting, you will likely feel tired. If you are reading on a laptop or smartphone, it may run out of battery. Getting tired and your device running out of battery are two very similar things. Both you and the device are complex systems that require this mysterious 'energy' stuff to function. The law of conservation of energy states that energy can neither be created nor destroyed, but it does come in many different forms such as electrical, mechanical, chemical, thermal and nuclear, and it can be converted between them.

For instance, you're powered by chemical energy, whereas your device uses electrical energy. However, the battery that powers your device is not storing electrical energy. It stores chemical energy, which is converted to electrical energy on demand. It does this by using electrodes and electrolytes. If the word 'electrolytes' sounds familiar, that's because it's in bold text on the front of most sports drinks. While your body stores chemical energy and uses it to contract muscles and move around, it's your brain that tells your body where to go by sending electrical energy through your nervous system to specific muscles at precise times. The chemical energy in your body is required to do everything, and the electrical energy tells your body what and when to do things. Chemical energy is the car, and electrical energy is the road it can travel on. If you look at the circuit board of a computer, it is essentially a network of tiny roads for electrical energy to flow through. *This is because all energy is only potential until it's given direction.* Therefore, wherever there is energy, you will find a director, for want of a better word.

This 'brains and brawn' dynamic often shows up in life: bow and arrow; gun and bullet; track and train; pilot and plane; citizens and government. I will later explain one instance of it related to money, using the terms 'layer-one energy' and 'layer-two energy', where layer one is the brawn (muscle) and layer two is the brains. I promise this does relate to Bitcoin.

Batteries

Imagine you are living in a world without batteries, and in this world you have two things:

1. A light bulb.

2. Exactly enough energy to power the light bulb, with no energy left to spare.

If you switch off that light bulb in this hypothetical world, your energy can't be used for anything else, so it must be streamed directly to the light bulb lest you waste your energy. This is great ... if you need to illuminate a room. But what if you need to boil a kettle? Let's assume it's a standard 100-watt light bulb; this would mean that powering the light bulb would require 100 joules of energy every second.

Since we have access to that energy requirement, we have 360,000 joules of energy to stream per hour. However, the average kettle uses 3,000 joules of energy per second when boiling water. So, if we were to hook up our power source to the kettle, it wouldn't be enough to bring the water to a boil. If you're anything like me, this is terrible news because, although they're few and far between, coffee is responsible for about 90 per cent of my life's greatest achievements, so to miss out on my morning coffee would be a disaster of biblical magnitude. Get your thinking caps on because we need to fix this.

If we have a steady stream of 100 joules per second, then we have 8,640,000 joules delivered to our house per day. Unless you sleep with the light on (no judging here), we aren't using the light bulb for the eight hours while we are asleep; so, we are wasting 2,880,000 joules of our energy allowance per day. If we had a way to re-route the energy stream to an energy storage device whenever the light bulb isn't in use, we would be able to store those joules of energy for later use, boiling more than enough water to fuel our somewhat-questionable coffee addiction!

Light bulbs can't backflip

I'm sure you're asking something along the lines of 'This is a chapter about the essence of money. Why is he talking about kettles and stuff?' Okay, I'll get to the point. Energy and money, as it turns out, aren't so different from one another; they are both quantifiable amounts of something that has the power to influence the actions of things in the material world, whether it be a kettle or a person. For instance, energy derived from food powers humans by providing the body and brain with the energy to do complex tasks such as thinking, digesting, walking, etc. You can think of this as layer-one energy. It's like the muscle; without it, we wouldn't be able to do anything at all. Then you have layer-two energy: the director. Desire happens in the brain, and it's a significant factor in a complex decision-making process that determines what you do with your time and energy.

Here's an example: eating an apple will give you about 100 kcals worth of energy (the unit of measurement for energy in food). This will provide about 116 watts (116 joules per second) if you eat an apple every hour. Funnily enough, you will run on 116 joules of energy for one second — about the same time as a lightbulb. Yes, it takes the same energy to power a human being as a light bulb. Granted, I've never met a coffee-dependent light bulb, but I don't remember the last time I saw a light bulb do a backflip, so that's a win for humanity as far as I'm concerned. Still, that raises two questions:

1. Why would anyone ever want to do a backflip?

2. Seriously … why would anyone ever want to do a backflip?

Desire is a complex idea; why does anyone ever want to do anything? It's a question I imagine light bulbs are unburdened by, but it's very relevant to humans. If you asked Austrian neurologist Sigmund Freud, he would've probably told you that humans desire that which increases their perceived potential as a sexual mate by their peers. If you asked evolutionary biologist Richard Dawkins, he would likely tell you that humans desire that which increases the likelihood of the gene pool resembling their genetic makeup down the line (such as cosmetic make-up, pun intended).

Regardless of why you believe humans want things, we want them, and we will do things we don't particularly want to do, so long as it means getting something we want in equal or greater proportions in return — unfortunately for most people, that's just called a job. However, the desirability of something is subjective, making it hard to measure in a standardised way. For now, I will lean on the idea of value, a concept that proposes the existence of an inherent and unwritten desirability/undesirability score attributed to every item or situation. If only we had some standardised way to put a number on this 'value' metric ... hmm.

Incentives

Don't get me wrong, humans often act altruistically, for one reason or another. Still, in the example of a tedious job, we do something like flipping burgers at McDonald's all day because we are given something at the end. Little pieces of paper with numbers on them. Society's token of acknowledgement for your hard work. We can then ask a favour from somebody else, maybe ask someone to deploy their hard work on one of our problems, for example: asking someone to give us a product (that took hard work to create) or to spend a few hours fixing our car.

Back-scratching and cash-grabbing

Most people would decline these requests unless you offer to give your 'work tokens' to them so that their contribution of value to greater society is *recorded*. This ensures that other members of society will provide them with products/services of equal value in return, and so on and so forth until we have an economy of accessible trade. In this example, the 'work tokens' you offer are the *incentive* for the other worker to help you. Incentives will be discussed a lot throughout this book, so whenever you read 'incentive', think of it as a psychological magnet that either pulls someone towards doing something (an incentive) or pushes them away from it (a disincentive).

Charging

To use a battery, you first must use electrical energy to charge it. You do this because you trust that the energy you expended to charge the battery will be redeemable in the future. Similarly, to spend money, you must first 'charge' your money (normally via a bank account) with the human energy you use to earn it. You also do this because you trust that the energy or value you expended to earn it will remain redeemable in the future. In this sense, money is an energy storage device, not of chemical energy or electrical energy, but of something I will call 'monetary energy', which encompasses both human energy and the value it produces. Where electrical energy can influence the actions of electrons, monetary energy can influence the actions of humans. It can do this because it's a constant incentive; everyone wants money. I will use the term 'monetary batteries' when discussing money to emphasise this core principle of money.

Tokens

Creating a standardised and measurable incentive technology to record the movement of value throughout members of a society (such as 'work tokens') serves two purposes: to put an agreed-upon numerical value on the desirability of goods and services to avoid resorting to inefficient barter, and to allow for a society to organise and cooperate on large-scale tasks that would otherwise be unachievable by any single person. We are all familiar with the first use case of measuring desirability. We use it every time we go food shopping and compare the prices of various products. Our energy from food (layer-one energy) is used for labour and exchanged for money (layer-two energy). Then we use that layer-two energy to provide our bodies with more layer-one energy by buying food. By comparing prices, we maximise the efficiency of that layer-one energy usage, hoping that we have some extra layer-two energy (money) left over.

We can't all be mechanics

The idea here is that we can exchange the remaining money for the layer-one energy and labour of other members of society. This is a brilliant idea because we can choose people who have proficiencies in areas outside our expertise. For example, hiring a mechanic to fix our car rather than learning to do it ourselves is a better idea since the energy required to learn how, and then do it ourselves, would be vastly more significant. Chances are, you would still do a worse job than the mechanic. Counter-intuitively, it works out *cheaper* for you to *pay* them. If the phrase 'cheaper to pay them' sounds weird, that's a good indicator of the disconnect between our modern understanding of money and its true purpose. In summary: money is to the economy what the scoreboard is to a basketball game: simply record-keeping technology.

Layer-two batteries

I'm sure you are now beginning to understand why I spent the first few paragraphs talking about light bulbs and batteries: you are the light bulb, food is the energy, and money is the battery. Without money, you would only ever use your energy to benefit yourself and your immediate social circle; this would hugely limit the potential of humanity. Without large-scale societal cooperation and organisation, there would be no skyscrapers, computers, businesses, medicine or modern civilisation. A house requires more than just a light bulb to make a home.

Humans are strictly bound to our incentives. Incentives decide what we do with our time and energy; if there's no incentive to do something, we won't do it. Money allows us to work on other people's projects with any excess energy that isn't immediately required for survival, while still storing that energy in a layer-two battery called money. It's a battery for value, which can then be given to other members of society in exchange for a comparable amount of value. In other words, it's a means for cooperation, and it immensely increases our capacity to progress as a species.

From house to home

The light bulb was wasting energy when it was switched off, and we would waste energy if we tried to be a jack-of-all-trades and build our own houses, find ourselves food, set up our own internet, build our own computers, etc. We simply wouldn't be capable. Cooperation made career specialisation possible by allowing farmers to focus entirely on farming while hunters concentrated on hunting, without either of them going hungry. This turned money into a battery for human labour that optimises the entire species' energy efficiency and productive output. It made value storable and portable.

2
Monopoly money

Okay, so ... I hope the first chapter has helped us get on the same page about what money is, using the best metaphor I can: monetary batteries. I use this metaphor because it highlights two core properties that money has: store of value and scarcity.

Store of value

This first property, 'store of value', is arguably the most fundamental attribute of money, and it combines two subcomponents: a function and a feature. The function is referred to by the word 'store', and the feature by the word 'value'. Value is often intersubjective; dollars have value because we all agree that they do. However, to store that value, the item's perceived value must be maintained over time, and a large part of that equation is scarcity; how many of these things exist?

Scarcity

Many people tend to make the mistake of thinking that scarcity determines value directly, but that's not the case. Increasing the available supply of something reduces its value — you've known this since you were a child playing with trading cards in primary school because the rarity of the cards *determined* their value. But oxygen isn't scarce at all, the supply is almost infinite, yet we still value it greatly. This is where we begin to separate the concept of *value* from *price*. If the world suddenly got the news that five years from now, oxygen levels in the atmosphere will be reduced by half, and we will all need to use pure oxygen inhalers to survive, then (as seen with the mid-pandemic toilet-roll hoarding catastrophe of 2020) the price of those oxygen inhalers would skyrocket.

Similarly, if the world got the news that we were about to mine an asteroid full of twice the Earth's gold reserves, then (as seen with the mid-pandemic oil-surplus catastrophe of 2020), the price of gold would fall.

The practical value of oxygen and gold remains the same in both examples: oxygen remains breathable, and gold remains a useful metal. Yet, by increasing or reducing the scarcity of those items, we can change their price by causing an auction-house-style bid for the item, where the highest bidder determines the price.

In the case of the oil surplus of 2020, there was a sudden reduction in the use of motor vehicles and other oil-fuelled machinery due to lockdowns, but oil production remained the same. More barrels of oil were being produced than the demand for oil could handle, so the price ended up *below* zero dollars. Yes ... negative. Companies were *paying* people to take barrels of oil off their hands.

How inflation works

Money is a battery for value; it is not value in and of itself. Like all batteries, it must be charged to serve its purpose. Have you ever been asked by someone, 'How much do you charge for your services?' You resist working for them because it takes time and energy, but their money has the power to convince you otherwise. This happens to be almost the exact definition of energy in physics: the capacity or ability to cause work to be done.

The laws of physics are pretty strict, particularly the one which states: 'Energy cannot be created nor destroyed.' So, what happens if you attempt to create more monetary energy, not by converting human energy to it, but by simply printing more money? The same thing happens when you try to make more pizza by cutting it into more slices: you end up with smaller slices. This is the first law of thermodynamics, a field of science that looks at many things, including the way heat transfers through and between objects. If you have a bucket of hot water and pour a cup of room-temperature water into it, you will end up with more hot water in total, but you won't end up with more heat. Similarly, if a country has x amount of money and then prints more, they will end up with more money in total, but they won't end up with more monetary energy. This is because the new money they printed is 'cold'. It's empty. It's like a battery without charge.

> Nature abhors a vacuum
> Aristotle

If we end up with the same amount of monetary energy after new money is added to the economy, what's the big problem? When you pour cold water into a bucket of hot water, it doesn't instantly change the temperature of it. Each water molecule needs to touch another molecule to absorb its heat. In an economy, this happens too. 'Cold' money doesn't get distributed instantly, or evenly. It's first given to the financial sector, thus affording them the privilege of spending it first, usually on assets and investments. As demand for these assets increases, their prices increase too. However, this happens long before your average Joe gets his hands on any of that new money. So, the monetary energy, the power that his money holds, is taken away.

For example, John, working one hour on minimum wage in the year 2000 in the UK, would have made £3.60. So, let's say one hour of human labour was equivalent to 3.6 monetary batteries. Today, in 2022, the minimum wage is £9.50, so John, having saved his £3.60, wouldn't get 30 minutes' worth of work for it. Over half of the energy John stored in those 3.6 batteries has gone — it's been drained. The battery is broken.

The number one cause of death... for nations

The central bank does not distribute newly printed money evenly. Much of it gets given directly to the financial sector and corporations, mainly in the form of very cheap loans. This simple process of governments creating money to stimulate more spending is hubristically called 'quantitative easing' in a glorious show of insider-speak. These names are almost always unnecessarily complicated and are usually replaceable with more straightforward terms. In this case, 'money printing' will do just fine. Easily accessible money and cheap loans increase spending in the economy. Creating money and lending it to companies means that the companies receiving the loan now have extra money to invest in themselves, be that through hiring more employees, buying more parts for production, or purchasing property to expand the company. As you can imagine, all this demand for goods/services drives prices up due to the law of supply and demand. This means that governments can drive demand in the economy during money-printing periods and incentivise spending. Hence, money printing usually happens during a recession, where a lack of spending is causing asset prices to fall.

Simple solutions to complex problems

This sounds great then, right? Surely this is just a brilliant way for governments to give the economy a 'kick into gear'? Unfortunately, that metaphor might be a bit too accurate. In practice, quantitative easing is very similar to giving the top of your TV a good slap when it's not working. It might fix it, but only temporarily. It's a plaster on the symptom, not a cure for the disease. When economies are undergoing recessions, printing money helps stock prices increase dramatically. With fast, easy money comes more spending and corporate expansion. With this corporate expansion, companies seem to be doing better on paper, inspiring confidence in their shareholders and thus increasing their stock price, and with this newfound sense of financial abundance permeating through society, we start spending. Thereby money starts changing hands faster, increasing the effective available supply of money in tandem with the demand for goods and services. As you can imagine, this is a recipe for massive price increases across the board.

With the cost of everything increasing, the initial sense of financial gain induced by the original hike in stock prices is called back into question, and to avoid an economic meltdown, central banks print more money. This is addiction.

Never out of the woods

Asset prices increasing is a good thing, though, right? Well, it depends. The wealthiest 1 per cent of Americans owned 38 per cent of all the value in the American stock market as of 2019, so the benefits of money printing seem to be mainly exclusive to the 'haves' rather than the 'have-nots'; asset prices increasing is only a good thing if you own assets. This brings up a serious question about money printing and wealth inequality.

Oh, and if you do own assets, put your wellies back on, you're not out of the woods yet. Money printing is only one factor of inflation. The best way to measure it is to simply check the money supply. If you're happy about your rising assets, I hate to be the bearer of bad news, but when measured against the supply of money, the line is so horizontal that flat-earthers are jealous. Basically, your assets aren't going up in value, but the value of the currencies they're measured against is just decreasing. The price of any asset is simply a division problem. The cost of apples in dollars is apples *divided* by dollars. So, if you want it to look like the price of apples is going up, you can just reduce the value of the denominator. The US stock market sharply rose 30 per cent following the coronavirus market crash, but so did the supply of money: coincidence? Maybe the value of stocks didn't increase. Perhaps the value of their price denominator just decreased.

Buying money

It's commonplace to refer to the provider of goods as the 'seller' and the provider of money as the 'buyer'. However, these terms just help us talk about trading more simply, so that you always know who is providing the goods and who is providing the money. In reality, both exchange participants buy something and sell something to acquire it. The 'seller' is buying money with goods, and the 'buyer' is buying goods with money. The term 'price' often refers to the amount of money required to purchase goods, but you can flip this on its head and use goods to price money. For instance, an ounce of gold has always been able to buy a decent suit. This is such a well-known fact that it has a name: 'Gold-to-Decent-Suit ratio'. An ounce of gold in 1967 Canada was worth about $35; the same amount of money would buy a nice suit from Eaton's department store. In 1975, the price of gold was $100, the same price as a decent suit from the same store. The cost of an ounce of gold, measured in suits, has always been about one, and the price of a suit, measured in gold, has always been about one ounce. Do you see where I'm going with this? Money is not outside the laws of supply and demand. It is a product like anything else, and it's here to serve several purposes: to provide information about labour allocation, store value, and facilitate exchange. This concept of pricing money in goods is often referred to as 'purchasing power' and asks: 'How much can I buy, per unit of a given currency?'

Language of value

Suits and gold haven't become more valuable since 1967, yet the price of gold has increased to over $1,700 per ounce as of writing (up from $37 in 1967). Because money is our language for communicating value, gold and suits must have just become more valuable? Not quite. Our language has been altered, like a game of Chinese Whispers for value where prices get slightly altered each year until the original meaning has been completely replaced with a new one. This is what you know of as 'inflation' and has completely ruined people's livelihoods in Venezuela, Zimbabwe, Sudan, Lebanon, Argentina, etc. The list is uncomfortably extensive. I would go so far as to say it includes almost every country that has ever existed in the past couple of thousand years.

3
How did we get here?

Okay, so ... quick recap:

1. Money is a method for storing value produced by labour in a portable and re-deployable way.

2. This ensures that a civilisation can cooperate and organise on a large scale.

3. Money is not outside the law of supply and demand; money itself is a product that serves a purpose.

4. The product (think 'money') that best serves that purpose will be used by society.

5. Today's money is incapable of maintaining its value over time; excessive creation of new 'empty' money has altered the way we understand and communicate value.

6. The urge to turn on the money printer has been too strong for any country thus far to avoid.

But how did we find ourselves in this mess? In 1921, £100 had the same purchasing power as £5,021 has in 2022. That means that the British pound has lost a shocking

98 per cent of its purchasing power since the Roaring Twenties. If you had found a fortune and buried it in your garden for your great-grandkids, it would barely pay for the shovel when they dug it up. This has a lot of harmful effects, but I'd like to quickly go over how we ended up where we are today.

I got what you want

The rise of the first agricultural revolution (circa 10,000 BC) saw humans transitioning from hunter-gathering to cultivating the land and farming our food rather than chasing it. This gave rise to specialisation: it's better to have a population of 50 great farmers and 50 great fishermen than 100 people who do a lousy job at both. However, since the farmers own the vegetables and the fishermen own the fish, it also accelerated trade. Not every farmer wants to live on broccoli, and I'm sure the fishermen would appreciate the odd barley beer.

Trade of this nature requires something called a 'coincidence of wants'. A sort of 'I want what you got, and you want what I have ...' scenario. But this wasn't always the case. A farmer can only harvest crops in season and, without refrigeration, his goods will only stay fresh for a limited time. So, he can't trade with anyone for a large portion of the year. We need a 'third good' that doesn't go bad or corrode, something everyone wants and will be willing to trade with throughout all seasons of the year. Introducing: money!

I got what we both want

Money has taken many forms throughout history; it was cows (scarce, but don't last very long), alcohol (scarce, lasts longer, but only if you don't drink it) and, most notably, cowrie shells for thousands of years. Cowrie shells were durable, pretty for jewellery, and very hard to find for most of human history, so they weren't vulnerable to inflation. Eventually, people realised that precious metals were almost perfect for use as money. Initially, silver was the dominant metal used as money because gold was too hard to find without adequate mining tools. But soon enough, gold became the symbol of wealth we know it as today. More labour was allocated to the production of gold, and the supply became large enough to make gold coins. So, the Lydian King Croesus minted the first gold coin with standardised purity for circulation circa 550 BC. The Roman Empire significantly advanced the science of mining, and by the height of their reign, circa AD 117, Roman coins spanned from Britain to North Africa. Global money had been invented, and international trade was possible like never before.

I got ... some paper?

Every form of money I just mentioned is known as commodity money. Commodity money is where the value of the commodity used for trade is in the item itself. It is easy to trust the value of gold or alcohol because they have intrinsic value. It feels secure and reasonable. But what if someone were to water down the liquor or melt the gold and mix it with other metals so there is less gold inside, and then recast it and pass it on as if it had the same purity? (This is often done by the person supposed to be responsible for ensuring it never happens.) It's known as debasement (a term you will hear a lot from Bitcoin enthusiasts) and isn't the only issue with commodity money. The second issue is the weight. Commodities are heavy, and if your economy grows you will eventually be making bigger deals that would require vast amounts of heavy commodities to be transported long distances to complete your payment, which can become very risky. Well then ... what do we do about this? We know why we need money: we need it to keep a record of human labour and contribution of value in a way that facilitates trade without resorting to inefficient barter. But we don't want to keep lugging around bags of gold that could potentially be counterfeit, debased or stolen from us.

The birth of currency

In around AD 800, under the Tang dynasty, the people of China were depositing their gold coins to trustworthy third parties that would give receipts of ownership on paper. Soon enough, instead of trading with actual gold, they began to trade the receipts for the gold instead, and those notes could be redeemed for gold later. They called it *Feipiao*, which means 'flying cash'. However, it wasn't until 1265 that the Song dynasty became the first society to create a truly national currency, a standardised paper-money system usable across the entire empire.

Fourteen years later, Kublai Khan and the Mongols conquered China and established the Yuan dynasty, creating their own purely paper currency unbacked by gold called the *chao*. They showed it to Venetian explorer Marco Polo, who was shocked by the idea of a purely paper currency.

This was the first unbacked paper money in human history. However, the experiment ultimately failed, of course, when the urge to print money became too strong for the Yuan dynasty to resist, leading to hyperinflation. Soon afterwards, the Ming dynasty tried it too, leading to much the same end. Before factory-printed money, counterfeiting was a much bigger problem; where American bills today say 'In God We Trust', the world's first paper money said 'Those who are counterfeiting will be decapitated'.

Breadwinner paperwinner

We took a break from paper money for a while, but eventually, Britain found itself in the middle of a war with France in 1688. Predictably, by the year 1694, they established the Bank of England to help fund it by issuing, you guessed it — paper money. A 'Gold Standard' emerged where paper money was freely interchangeable with gold at a decided rate. The United Kingdom became the first country to formally adopt the gold standard in 1821. Any paper money that did exist before the mid-1800s was more like certificates of gold-coin deposits to banks, handwritten and signed by the cashier. That was until 1853, the year that Great Britain made their first entirely printed banknote without the signature of a cashier. Nine years later, the United States followed suit. This marked the beginning of a new 'monetary gold' economy. Paper notes were still convertible to precious metal coins, and by the year 1900, an international gold standard was established and adopted by most countries. This remained true until the First World War.

The 100-year-old reason you can't pay your rent

Suppose you are a government that has successfully created an economy where the population is happy to work for printed paper bills. You suddenly find yourself smack-dab in the middle of a world war. You'll need all the funding you can get to ensure that you come out on top. This is where countries began to 'temporarily' suspend their adhesion to the gold standard and, as economist Milton Friedman said, 'Nothing is so permanent as a temporary government programme.'

This quote proved entirely accurate; after the First World War ended, many countries were left with notes that couldn't be converted to gold or silver. Foreign exchange rates between currencies became volatile, and higher inflation inevitably led to the Great Depression in 1929. Friedman's quote became painfully true in 1933 when the United States asserted that they were breaking up with gold in a totalitarian 'Dear John' letter called Executive Order 6102, which *criminalised* the ownership of monetary gold. It remained a crime to own monetary gold until the mid-1970s — but this law did not apply to the government. In 1944, the United States got back together with gold at a romantic conference in Bretton Woods, New Hampshire, and the rest of the world followed suit. Humanity and gold lived happily ever after ... until 1971.

Bretton Woods

After the Second World War, representatives from 44 countries met at Bretton Woods to discuss monetary policy. Eventually, they agreed on a system where the

United States dollar (USD) would act as the world's reserve currency rather than gold and that the USD would be convertible to gold at a fixed rate. They called it the Bretton Woods system. The world was back on a gold standard, albeit by taking a detour through dollars to arrive there. However, 11 years later, America had fought the Korean War, the Cold War had long begun, the Vietnam War was heating up and military spending was through the roof. Naturally, they began printing dollars ... I'm guessing you can see where this is going. The dollar's devaluation spread to other countries that held dollar reserves and as if the dollar was a stock, countries began planning to sell theirs for gold. America wasn't happy about this because they had printed so many dollars that they no longer had the gold reserves to back it up. They had violated the primary rule of Bretton Woods: peg the value of the US dollar to the value of gold.

America attempted to persuade the world that they didn't want gold and that what they truly wanted, like, deep, deep down, was pieces of paper with photos of US presidents on them. However, devaluing the dollar wasn't the most persuasive action.

1971

So, what did America do? In 1971, President Richard Nixon temporarily paused the convertibility of dollars to gold, essentially saying, 'Nah ...' to countries requesting their gold. If there is one thing you have learned from this chapter, it's that nothing is so permanent as a temporary government programme. The gold standard has been gone ever since, and the dollar has lost 86 per cent of its value. The amount of dollars in existence has increased from

600 billion in 1971 to over 21,000 billion today. That's an additional $20 trillion! To put that into perspective, if you were to earn $60 a minute for every single minute since the first *Homo sapiens* emerged, you would only have made *half* of the dollars that exist today.

4
Database culture

Remember in the previous chapter when I said: 'We know why we need money'? In order to to *keep a record* of human labour to facilitate trade without resorting to inefficient barter. And I pointed out the undesirability of lugging around bags of gold that could potentially be counterfeit, debased, or stolen. This highlights the two primary realisations that lead to paper money:

1. **Money is only needed to keep a record of labour and production of value.**

2. **Commodities inefficiently keep that record.**

I've attempted to describe what money is using the metaphor of a monetary battery that stores humans' societal value contribution in a portable form. Buried inside that metaphor is also the *purpose* that money serves, namely, to quantify value according to a standardised unit of measurement that everyone agrees upon. This way, when I spend £20 at Top Joe's pizza, Joe's production of pizza-shaped value is recorded when he's left with £20 in his account. Conversely, my *consumption* of value is recorded when £20 leaves my account. That's why it's called an account; it *accounts* for value *measured* in British pounds. Money is not the economy; the economy is goods and services — i.e. value — and money is a measurement system for *quantifying* that value.

Record-keeping

At this point, we have established the position of money as record-keeping technology. However, labour allocation is only one thing we need to keep a record of. Google needs to pay its employees for sacrificing their time and energy to maintain the company, but they also need to keep a record of their customers, sales, supply chain, imports, etc. And, as we all know, recording customer data is where the prize lies.

Before modern technology, customer data was scarce and undetailed. However, with modern technology, we can collect mountains of customer data and analyse precisely what advertisements they respond to best, creating more customers and even more data. It's a self-perpetuating cycle.

Nowadays, because customers grow in numbers exponentially, big tech companies are finding ways to solidify the average consumer's loyalty. When was the last time you ever used Yahoo! or Bing as your search engine? The grip that Google has over the internet is so strong that I can't even ask you about its competitors without mentioning its name. The word 'google' is officially a verb in the dictionary.

The world is vulnerable to monopolies, primarily thanks to a single invention by IBM in the 1970s, which revolutionised the world more than we can ever imagine.

Sequel? No, SQL

Money is simple record-keeping: if I pay John £10, I subtract £10 from my account balance and add £10 to his. But what if I wanted to keep a record of every health check-up and doctor's appointment for all 66,000,000 citizens of the UK? Well, that's not just maths. It's information regarding various aspects of health, so we need somewhere to put multi-categorical information. I'm talking columns, rows, names, keys, more columns, and even more rows … we need a spreadsheet.

Before computers, the primary record-keeping technology was paper and filing cabinets. This is subject to the same problems commodity money faced: it's heavy; large; vulnerable to single points of failure; flammable (seriously … that sucks); human-error prone, partially due to inconsistent layouts; it's hard to audit and maintain version history, etc. The list goes on. Then, during the 1970s, IBM revolutionised record-keeping with Structured Query Language, or 'SQL'. SQL is a computer programming language that allowed us to create massive databases with an unlimited number of rows and columns. On top of that, we could query, edit and perform complex operations on that data at will — no more pesky paper.

Where Excel doesn't excel

These days, both you and I work with some format of digital databases every day. When you log in to an account online, check in at the gym or send your friend money online, you're using digital databases. It could be said that digital databases are one of the (if not *the*) most important technological innovations of the past 100 years.

The invention of the digital database has revolutionised banking, finance, science, business, etc. Even while you are scrolling through Facebook, you are feeding a database, and this is where we begin to encounter problems. These days, advancements in data science have made data one of the most valuable commodities in the world.

> You're not the customer, you're the product.
> Richard Serra

Social media is free because how you use it is recorded. Your interests are analysed, and that data is used for advertising products you might want or need. Data science is now so advanced (thanks to artificial intelligence) that tech companies may know you want or need something *before* you know it yourself. An anecdote of an angry father: after receiving coupons for pregnancy products addressed to his teen daughter from the US retail giant Target in the mail, he complained to the company that they were encouraging his teen daughter to get pregnant. A couple of days later, he called and apologised, stating that his daughter had discovered she was pregnant. The retailer's statistician, Andrew Pole, worked on a 'pregnancy prediction' score, which tracked customers browsing/buying products and assigned them a pregnancy likeliness score based on purchasing behaviour; this was then used to market baby products to newly pregnant women. It happened to work so well that the retailer knew this girl was pregnant *before* her father.

Times a billion

That's just from analysing product purchases at one retailer. Imagine what you could do if you knew somebody's search history, browsing behaviour, what online media they consume and how long they pay attention to each type of media, what ads they skip, what ads they watch, what political commentaries they pay attention to, what products they buy?

Multiply that by billions of daily internet users and store all that data on centralised databases, and you have a severe problem on your hands. Not just because the data could be used with evil intent, but when data becomes the primary driver of profits, you have a 'non-cooperative game theory' at play.

In game theory, this is defined as a competitive game type where resources are hoarded rather than shared. When data is the resource, you have 'asymmetric information theory' at play. In a situation of asymmetric information, one participant in a transaction possesses more information about the transaction than the other, allowing the exploitation of the uninformed party or parties.

Today, one example of asymmetric information comes in the form of big data, which incentivises non-cooperative action among corporations. For example, corporations obscure aspects of their supply-chain operations to maximise their dominance over the marketplace at the expense of the less fortunate. Child labour is a prime example.

I must clarify here; I am well aware that competition is a principal function of free-market economies. *Non-cooperation does not equal non-competitiveness.* Cooperation is the substructure on which competition is predicated; to compete you must agree on the parameters of the game. A game of chess is cooperative because mutual conformity to the rules of chess is *chess*. That is what *qualifies* chess as chess ... hence why cheaters get *dis-qualified*; their lack of cooperation means they no longer qualify as competitors in the game. Thus, non-cooperative action among corporations disintegrates free-market economics by virtue of being the antithesis of competition.

Stuck in the middle with ... everyone else?

This centralised form of digital database that I'm referring to can have off-site backups, but all the data is often stored in a single location at any given backup site. We no longer have commodity money's 'weight' or 'size' problem, but the issue of the singular point of failure remains. This proved hugely problematic when the company Cambridge Analytica harvested the personal data of 87 million people from Facebook. They used it to create psychologically-tailored political propaganda in the form of Facebook posts/ads that appeared in targeted user feeds to 'alter behaviour' during elections across the world. Through artificial intelligence fuelled data analysis, inspired by the world of the military psychological operations specialists that worked for Cambridge Analytica parent company, SCL Group. Unfortunately, for the artificial intelligence giant, the public didn't take too kindly to them meddling around with global politics when the story inevitably went public in 2018.

Game theory of database culture

Cyber-war threats incentivise governments to arm themselves with software exploits (hacks). One software exploit was 'EternalBlue', developed by the US National Security Agency (NSA) to 'attack' a vulnerability in Microsoft's implementation of SMB (a remote-access file-sharing protocol). Due to the 'single point of failure' aspect of database culture, the NSA database containing EternalBlue was itself the target of a cyberattack. As a result, EternalBlue was leaked to the public.

The WannaCry ransomware attack used EternalBlue to access over 300,000 computers worldwide. The attackers then encrypted those computers, rendering them useless, and held them to ransom. The National Health Service (NHS) in the UK was hit the hardest, with MRI scanners, blood-storage refrigerators and theatre equipment being affected, causing non-critical emergencies to be turned away and ambulances to be diverted. Damage estimates range from hundreds of millions up to four billion dollars globally.

Additionally, due to the 'non-cooperative game theory' aspect of database culture, the NSA, which at the time had known about Microsoft's vulnerability for five years, had never alerted Microsoft. A storm was brewing.

The good with the bad

Technological advancement is no easy feat. New technologies are just the first iteration of what's to come later, and databases are no different. Although digital database technology has been immensely beneficial for the *efficiency* and *security* of humanity, it comes at the cost of centralised single points of failure across multiple industries and has many inefficiencies of its own.

Almost everything that humans venture to achieve requires efficient and reliable record-keeping. The record-keeping technology that best fulfils those two parameters will prosper because the destiny of humankind depends on it.

Part two:
What is Bitcoin?

5
Blockchain culture

Life for cavemen looked a lot different than it did for the Romans. I don't think anyone would dispute that, but why is that the case?

Well, technology changed immensely between those periods. The technological change caused that change in living standards. Technology even caused that technology change. It took *Homo sapiens* over 200,000 years to develop the first working aeroplane ... 66 years later, we walked on the moon. Today, the computers inside our phones are 100,000 times more powerful than those used to send us there. Technological growth is exponential, humans are resourceful, and we use technology to invent new technologies, from the hammer to the iPhone.

Turing

It wasn't until 1936 that Alan Turing laid down the theoretical basis for the computer as we know it, the first of which was built in 1945. To put that into perspective, if we were to condense human history into one year, the computer was invented six hours ago, the internet was invented two hours ago, and the iPhone emerged only 60 minutes ago … a lot has changed during that time. The internet was so revolutionary that it ushered in a new age of human history: the Information Age.

Hey! Networks exist now, and they're AWESOME

During the initial development of the internet, finding databases and documents online looked a lot like a file browser. You had to find the file you wanted, download it, and then open it using some file-reading application on your computer. This was not ideal, but it was early days. Then along came the worldwide web and the idea that your internet browser and file-reading software could be the same application. This turned the internet into a practical networking technology anyone could use, and boy, did we use it.

However, there's an issue: databases can't easily talk to each other. Maintaining multiple versions of the same database is an expensive struggle. Not to mention that if the server holding your data goes down, you may lose access entirely. Or, in the case of banking, sending money means the bank simply alters the balance associated with your name on their database, and so to send money you must first ask their permission to do it for you. You'll know this if you have ever tried to make an international payment on the weekend or bank holiday.

Since banks send your money on your behalf, you must also pay for their services. Additionally, they will take about 5 per cent of the foreign exchange rate. Banks have lots of leverage for this reason. If it weren't for physical cash (which governments are trying very hard to get rid of), we would be financially paralysed without banks. This leverage is what's known as a middleman position. If you want to give your friend £10, banks stand in the middle and do it for you while they tear a piece from the edge of the note. This may be an effective system but it is still not efficient.

When a database and a network love each other very much …

> **What's great about a database?**
> **It keeps a record of data.**
> **What's great about a network?**
> **It *distributes* data.**
> **What's the main problem with a database?**
> **It's like … super-duper *centralised*.**

Hmm, what's that old saying … opposites attract?

Amnesiac village

Let's imagine we have a small village of 100 people. These people live on an island far away from civilisation, so they've never heard of computers, and one morning they all wake up with total amnesia. They can't remember a thing. Not only that, but all their money has been stolen! However, they don't know this, of course, because they don't remember what money is. So they go on living. They barter for trade, and encounter all the same problems that ancient humans encountered before money was invented.

A couple of weeks later, they have taken on an 'I scratch your back, you scratch mine' way of life, based on reciprocity. However, disputes are becoming a regular occurrence, and

'I did you a favour, and you didn't return it!' is now a more common phrase than 'Good morning!' in the village. They are unconsciously developing a desire for a record-keeping system for labour when they discover a filing cabinet (don't ask why it took weeks to find a filing cabinet) with a paper-based system recording all the payments between each other that they had ever made before their money was taken and their memories wiped.

The ledger

This type of list that records transactions across time is called a ledger. The villagers' money was called 'soc', so every transaction on the ledger looked like: *'James, 1 S, Lucy'*. This meant that James had paid one soc to Lucy. However, as they don't remember that physical money ever existed, they just need to account for their labour and create a monetary battery. As far as they're concerned, the paper database has solved their problem. Thus, hoping they're rich, each person adds up their incomings and subtracts the sum of their outgoings to figure out their account balance, and they begin making some rules.

The protocol

Adding/making transactions

A payer must sign all their payments to validate ownership of their account. Every villager must maintain a personal copy of the ledger. Any new transaction must be shown to a villager to validate that the payer has the required funds. If they deem the transaction valid, they must record it to their copy of the ledger in a section dedicated to memorising the pool of unconfirmed transactions; let's call it the mem-pool for short. They must then show another villager, and so on, until the entire village is eventually aware of all new unconfirmed transactions.

Confirming transactions

They need a system to ensure that the history of transactions is the same on everyone's copy of the ledger, thus ensuring everyone agrees on who owns what. However, they can't give this responsibility to any single person, or group of people, because they could be corrupt or dishonest, or coerced into being so. To avoid this, all villagers must reach agreement on the true history of transactions *mutually*, and in a *decentralised* manner.

So, they devise a system where the villagers attend a meeting at the end of each day to *confirm* new transactions by adding them to the official ledger. Only once a transaction is added to the official ledger is it considered to be a confirmed transaction.

Once a transaction has been confirmed in this way, they erase it from the mem-pool, making space for new unconfirmed transactions to be written down. However, they can't simply take a majority vote on which transactions to confirm because a majority could conspire against a minority without punishment. So, they host a Rubik's Cube race every day and call the participants 'racers'. The first person to win the race chooses a bunch of unconfirmed transactions from the mem-pool, writes them on a new ledger entry, and adds it to the official ledger to collect a reward. This reward is a pre-agreed amount of money added to the account balance of whoever wins the race and confirms transactions, as well as optional transaction fees included in the transactions they chose to confirm.

Suppose they attempt to give themselves a bigger reward than previously agreed or enter any invalid transactions into the ledger. In that case, the rest of the villagers and Rubik's Cube racers will reject their entire entry to the ledger, they will have to start over, their reward will be lost, and the race will continue. This randomises and decentralises the authority of confirming transactions, favouring only those who put in the most time and energy to solve their Rubik's Cube; a group to whom ensuring the validity of transactions matters the most, lest they lose their reward.

The more competition there is to solve the Rubik's cube, the harder it becomes to win the race. The more effort you dedicate to winning, the less likely you are to try anything shady should you succeed, lest your efforts go to waste.

This system incentivises the collective maintenance and security of the ledger while reinforcing its decentralisation and providing rewards to the guardians of truth. Conversely, it punishes the traitors of truth by making corruption and dishonestly a futile, self-destructive endeavour.

The result

In the villagers' system, all payments are simply entries to a distributed ledger that everyone agrees upon. This state of agreement is called consensus. In this case, the consensus is reached *without* a central authority, so the system is a *de-centralised* consensus mechanism — a mouthful, I know.

If you swap the paper database for a digital one and swap the social network for a computer network, and add a pinch of fancy maths ... congratulations, you just invented a permissionless blockchain.

Returning to my original question, then: what happens when a database and a network love each other very much? They have a baby, and that baby is called distributed-ledger technology.

Tech and culture — an unbreakable bond

Undoubtedly, the technologies available to a civilisation dictate the cultural foundation of its people. The database revolution saw the phrase 'tech giants' become associated with data-harvesting corporate monopolies rather than cutting-edge technological innovation. The internet revolution turned 'website' from a novelty to a necessity, and where 'email' once described a complex technology, it now describes a morning routine.

The blockchain revolution will see the phrase 'digital money' turn from an oxymoron to an industry standard; the phrase 'corporate transparency' from a utopian daydream to an infrastructural attribute; the phrase 'financial restrictions' from an inescapable fact to an optional suggestion.

Now, I'm being optimistic, of course, but I'm young, and that's my job. Each of these things is hugely important. Digital money provides self-banking to the unbanked. Corporate transparency eliminates hidden child labour. Financial restrictions paralyse citizens of developing countries ... and that's just the tip of the iceberg.

Why it works

Blockchain is one form of distributed-ledger technology. It's very similar to the example of the amnesiac village: the villagers don't encounter any of the problems I have discussed so far.

1. They don't use commodity money, so the security and efficiency issues are eliminated.

2. They don't risk hyper-inflation because the supply of money is finite.

3. They don't need a middleman or trusted third party to pay each other, so there are no monopolistic banks.

4. They can't do dodgy deals because the ledger is public.

You get my point.

In effect, they have *extracted* the benefits of money *from* money, just as the United States tried to do in 1971, and they did it with no dependence on trust or central authority.

Now, imagine if you could computerise this entire process. I hope you're beginning to see why everyone is talking about blockchain.

6
Introducing Bitcoin

The world in the 2000s was unstable: we were 30 years into the post-Bretton Woods experiment, and the supply of US dollars was increasing. Mortgage-backed securities became the backbone of the economy, and, well ... 2008 showed us how that went.

By early 2009, headlines from newspapers such as *The Times's* from 3 January, 'Chancellor on brink of second bailout for banks', were a broken record. Later that day, an anonymous programmer added that headline to the first-ever entry of the Bitcoin ledger: *'The Times 03/Jan/2009 Chancellor on brink of second bailout for banks'*. At the time of writing, 709,270 entries have been added since that date, one every 10 minutes.

I hope that I have sufficiently illuminated the problem that money aims to solve and the issues that each form of money throughout history has been married to, and provided you with a fresh perspective on what money is, rather than just what it does. If you have endured all my historical and conceptual ramblings until this point, I applaud you, but it's time to get to the good stuff: how does this whole blockchain thing work, and what the hell is Bitcoin?

Evolution starts with a cell

Computers and information technology began with the abacus over 3,000 years ago. It was a great advance but still required the user to do most of the legwork. It wasn't until humans learned to manipulate electrical currents that things became interesting. Similarly, the first form of record-keeping technology emerged when a stone met the wall of a cave. Eventually, we ran out of writing space in the caves and mashed some plants and bark into super-thin slices to write on instead. Today we call this paper.

Still, the human population grew, and paper became increasingly problematic. So, the descendants of the abacus and the rock had a happy marriage to create the computerised database. Great, now we can record an infinite amount of data and 'do maths to it' too. Then came the new kid on the block, the computer network, who was very attractive and often went by the stage name 'Internet'. Internet married the computerised database (with the help of a little couples therapy from cryptography) to create Bitcoin. That's what Bitcoin is. Thank you for reading, *roll credits*. Okay, the liberties I took in artistic licence may have cost me some accuracy there, so let me redeem myself.

Genesis

The accolade of Bitcoin's invention is handed to the mysteriously aliased Satoshi Nakamoto, but this is useless because we have no idea who they are, or even if they are only one person. Although Bitcoin's genesis block was only created in 2009, and Satoshi only began appearing on chatrooms and internet forums a year prior, the idea of Bitcoin had already been long in the making.

Computers were becoming very popular during the 1980s, and some forward-thinking people were already predicting the potential threats to come in the following years, specifically concerning privacy.

In 1992, worried that the internet could become a battleground for freedom and privacy, American mathematician and computer programmer, Eric Hughes released *A Cypherpunk Manifesto* and founded the Cypherpunk email list, kickstarting the Cypherpunk movement.

The Cypherpunks were a niche group of computer geeks who believed that the internet would someday pose a threat to privacy and freedom. They were already contemplating the notion of a borderless digital cash system decades before you made your first email account, so I think it's safe to say that they were ahead of their time. However, they didn't just contemplate; they built. Yet there were many problems to overcome before they could invent a truly digital currency, the most prolific being the double-spend problem.

You can't have your money and spend it too

Bitcoin was not the first attempt at digital money. There were multiple attempts prior, nearly 20 years before the words 'bit' and 'coin' ever found a happy home. All such attempts were stifled by one major roadblock: the double-spend problem.

This is one of the core issues that prevented 'money' and 'digital' from inhabiting the same sentence before the 1980s. It goes something like this: physical money is good because if I give you my coin, the transaction is recorded, and the act of transacting prohibits me from spending that coin again unless I were to steal it back from you. This is what I mean when I refer to money as record-keeping technology; a transaction is recorded and finalised by its very occurrence.

However, this is a slight issue when you are designing a digital cash system. 'Digit-al' is precisely that: digits of information on a storage drive. Therefore, without having a central authority to decide what the truth is, nothing stops you from simply copy-pasting those digits and spending the duplicates, enabling you to have your money and spend it too. This would be a disastrous monetary network.

You can see how this was a seemingly insurmountable problem … until our friend Satoshi Nakamoto decided to emerge from the shadows.

Bitcoin's parents

David Chaum was perhaps the first to make a serious attempt at creating digital money. In 1982, already a pioneer in the field of anonymous digital communications, Chaum released the whitepaper for an algorithm he called 'eCash'. This was the first serious attempt at creating truly digital money.

In summary, it worked by using serial numbers assigned to each token. This signature would then be verified by a 'bank' to check whether a user had already spent the token. However, the role of the bank added a centralisation problem, and Chaum's company, DigiCash, filed for bankruptcy in 1998 after the rise of PayPal and less privacy-centric digital payments solutions.

Many other attempts occurred during this time, most notably the invention of e-gold, which amassed transfer volumes exceeding two billion dollars yearly. E-gold's solution was similarly centralised: gold backed the e-gold token's value. It's worth noting that somebody was responsible for the safety of all that gold. Before Bitcoin, the failings of digital money solutions can be summarised as a vulnerability to something called a Sybil attack.

Sybil cynicism

Digital money advocates, and pioneers of the pre-Bitcoin era, set their sights on solving the double-spend and distributed-consensus problem, only to be met with another, equally menacing problem: the Sybil attack. To solve the double-spend problem, you need a network capable of reaching consensus, and the most intuitive form of distributed consensus is a democracy. If it works for elections, a majority vote should also work for digital cash transactions, right?

Well, yes ... and no.

The issue here is that (unlike state-run elections) anonymous networks don't know the identities of their users. Without identification, there is no telling whether any cluster of accounts on the network are owned by multiple people or just one individual. Giving each account an equal share of voting rights could mean giving one person majority voting power over the network if they create enough accounts.

Progress wasn't easy; with every problem that was solved there were ten new issues, and digital money was seemingly impossible to 'invent'. Until along came an anonymous person who solved the anonymity problem. In fact, he didn't just solve the anonymity problem ... *he solved all the problems.*

I appreciate your questions. I actually did this
kind of backwards. I had to write all the code
before I could convince myself that I could solve
every problem, then I wrote the paper.
Satoshi Nakamoto, November 2008

Then there was the blockchain.

So, what exactly was so revolutionary about Bitcoin?
It introduced blockchain: a method for reaching
decentralised consensus on a distributed ledger that's
transparent, open-source, immutable and immune to the
double-spend problem, all while being entirely operated
and governed by its anonymous users. How blockchain
manages all this will blow your socks off, which leads us
nicely into the next chapter.

7

How does Bitcoin work? (and WTF is a blockchain?)

Before starting this chapter, I just need to define a word: hash. A hash, or a cryptographic hash, can be thought of like a smoothie. If you put a million fruits into a blender, you will still just get a smoothie. Swap just one of those fruits for something else, and you've changed the entire smoothie; even though most of the ingredients remain the same, it is a different smoothie at the end.

A cryptographic hash function works similarly: it takes in data, such as a file, and outputs a number in hexadecimal format (letters and numbers) that could only result from the exact data you inputted. If you were to hash the word 'hello' using the SHA256 hashing algorithm, it would return:

2CF24DBA5FB0A30E26E83B2AC5B9E29E
1B161E5C1FA7425E73043362938B9824

However, if you were to hash 'Hello' with a capital, it would return:

185F8DB32271FE25F561A6FC938B2E26
4306EC304EDA518007D1764826381969

No matter how insignificant, any change to the input will produce an entirely different result. The most crucial point here is that the same bowl of fruit will always turn into the same smoothie, yet you will never be able to turn the smoothie back into a bowl of fruit.

Regardless of the size of the input to SHA256, the output will always be the same size: 64 characters. Moreover, suppose you're talking to your friend, and you both claim to know a super-duper secret smoothie recipe. Neither of you wants to disclose the recipe to the other in case the other doesn't know the recipe and was just trying to gain smoothie secrets. In that case, you both could make a bottle of your secret smoothie, and if the smoothies taste the same, you can both be confident that the other person knows the secret recipe, all while never revealing the recipe at any point. Additionally, you only gave them a single bottleful (64 characters), so the number of fruits used (the input's size) can also remain a secret.

Talking of secrets, if you're worried that you won't understand how Bitcoin works after reading this chapter, don't be, because you already understand it; I secretly explained how Bitcoin works a couple of chapters ago because I knew you'd switch that big brain of yours off as soon as I mentioned mining or computer networks. Remember the amnesiac village? That's the Bitcoin network. If you replaced the following terminology:

— Villagers: **'nodes'**

— Ledger entries: **'blocks'**

— Official ledger: **'blockchain'**

— Rubik's Cube race: **'mining'**

- Rubik's Cube racers: **'miners'**

- Confirming transactions: **'mining a block'**

- Mem-pool: **'mempool'**

- End of each day: **'every ten minutes'**

- Effort: **'electricity'**

... and explained the amnesiac village system to a friend using those words instead, you would be explaining how Bitcoin works. That's not a joke, look:

Adding/making transactions:
A payer must sign all their payments to validate ownership of their account. Every **node** must maintain a personal copy of the **blockchain**. Any new transaction must be shown to a **node** to validate that the payer has the required funds. If they deem the transaction valid, they must record it to their copy of the **blockchain** in a section dedicated to **mem**orising the **pool** of unconfirmed transactions, let's call it the **mempool** for short. They must then show another **node**, and so on, until **all nodes are** eventually aware of all new unconfirmed transactions.

Confirming transactions:
We need a system to ensure that the history of transactions is the same on every **node's** copy of the ledger, thus ensuring every **node** agrees on who owns what. However, we can't give this responsibility to any single **node**, or group of **nodes**, because they could be corrupt or dishonest, or coerced into being so. To avoid this, all **nodes** must reach an agreement on the true history of transactions *mutually*, and in a *decentralised* manner. So, they devise a system where the **nodes** attend a meeting **every ten minutes** to

confirm new transactions by adding them to the **blockchain**.

Only once a transaction is added to the **blockchain** is it considered to be a confirmed transaction. Once a transaction has been confirmed in this way, they erase it from the **mempool**, making space for new unconfirmed transactions to be written down. However, they can't simply take a majority vote on which transactions to confirm because a majority could conspire against a minority without punishment. So, they host a **mining** race **every ten minutes** and call the participants '**miners**'. The first **miner** to win the race chooses a bunch of unconfirmed transactions from the **mempool**, writes them on a new **block**, and adds it to the **blockchain** to collect a reward. This reward is a pre-agreed amount of money added to the account balance of whoever wins the race and confirms transactions, as well as optional transaction fees included in the transactions they chose to confirm.

Suppose they attempt to give themselves a bigger reward than previously agreed or enter any invalid transactions into the **blockchain**. In that case, the rest of the **nodes** and **miners** will reject their entire **block**, they will have to start over, their reward will be lost, and the race will continue. This randomises and decentralises the authority of confirming transactions, favouring only those who put in the most **electricity** to **mining**, a group to whom ensuring the validity of transactions matters the most, lest they lose their reward. The more competition there is to **mine a block**, the harder it becomes to win the race. The more **electricity** you dedicate to winning, the less likely you are to try anything shady should you succeed, lest your **electricity** goes to waste.

The block

Whenever I say 'Bitcoin's blockchain', just imagine a version of the ledger in the amnesiac village that's instead maintained over email rather than paper. The 'block' part of blockchain refers to the list of recent transactions added to the ledger at the end of each day. The only difference is that with Bitcoin, a new 'block' (remember, it's just a list of transactions) is added to the blockchain roughly every 10 minutes.

The Bitcoin blockchain allows the size of blocks to be no larger than four megabytes (4 MB). However, assuming no significant changes to Bitcoin, we probably won't see a block larger than two megabytes (2 MB) for weird mathematical reasons that I won't get into ... but I digress. Because of this block size limit, each block holds approximately 2,000 transactions on average. At 2,000 transactions per block and one block every ten minutes, the transactions per second (TPS) of Bitcoin is limited. On average, Bitcoin handles between three and five transactions per second, causing the queue of unconfirmed transactions to grow. This may seem like a design fault, and it's a contentious topic of debate among crypto advocates, but it's very intentional. In the amnesiac village, if they allowed an infinite number of transactions to be added to the ledger each day, those transactions would end up occupying thousands of sheets of paper. Eventually, it would become impossible for the villagers to maintain personal copies of the entire ledger.

The anatomy of a block

When I first saw a block for myself, I found it quite helpful as it took the highly conceptual ideas into the real world. Feel free to skip past this part; it's just here to demystify blocks and remind you they are simply lists. Just like this one:

Header:

Contains general information about the block, including:

Block height: How many blocks there are before the current one.

Block size: The amount of data in the block, measured in bytes.

Block hash: The SHA256 encryption of all data in the block.

Version: The Bitcoin version used by the miner of the block.

Timestamp: Yeah ... it's just a timestamp.

Bits: The target threshold/maximum value that the hashed result of the block can return.

Nonce: A number added to the block to make the hashed result lower than the maximum.

hashPrevBlock: The hashed result of the previous block in the blockchain.

hashMerkleRoot: The encrypted sum of all transactions to verify their occurrence.

nTx: The total amount of transactions in the block.

Transactional data:

Block reward: The first transaction in the list, containing the reward afforded to the miner.

Transactions: A list of every transaction within the block and all their respective hashes.

The chain

As you can probably imagine, the 'chain' refers to the chain of entries to the ledger. Since every block added to the blockchain contains a cryptographic hash of the previous block, it's essentially a chain of blocks. In other words, each new list of transactions added to the ledger references the previous list, back to the first block ever created.

However, this isn't merely to keep everything in order. The data contained within the blockchain is primarily transactions: 'Alice sends Bob five Bitcoins', for example. The complete history of all transactions determines the account balance of every Bitcoin address. Thus, whoever controls the past, controls the present. Therefore, it's of paramount importance that the past cannot be altered, it must remain *immutable*, and the linkage of each block to its 'parent' and 'child' (previous and next) blocks ensures this.

Let me explain. If someone were to attempt to 'double-spend' by removing a payment they made from the official blockchain, it would alter the data contained within the block. Therefore, the hash of that block would change too. But wait! The hash of every block is contained within the next block, so the next block's hash would change too! So, if you tried to convince other nodes that your fraudulent block is legitimate, they would see that no blocks reference it. If no other blocks reference yours, it's either the most recent block or not part of the blockchain at all!

Security and Proof of Work

The monetary system adopted by the amnesiac villagers was entirely dependent on the code of conduct they implemented to ensure everyone stayed honest. Another word for code of conduct is 'protocol', so whenever you hear 'the Bitcoin protocol', it refers to the code of conduct to which Bitcoin participants must adhere. Instead of being written on paper, it's written in code.

There are two main parts to the security protocol implemented by the villagers:

1. Peers check the validity of new transactions before passing them on.

2. The Rubik's Cube race (mining) determines who adds unconfirmed transactions to the shared ledger.

Both occur within the Bitcoin protocol too. 'Nodes' verify new transactions, and 'miners' add them to the ledger. Nodes are the people in the village, listening for recent transactions, double-checking their validity and passing them on. These are the ones that put the liars in the 'naughty corner'. Miners (racers) are also nodes (villagers); they're just nodes that participate in the Rubik's Cube race as well. Miners compete for the right to add their list of unconfirmed transactions to the ledger.

The mining process is surprisingly straightforward; remember how each block has a hash? Well, mining is the process of choosing a bunch of unconfirmed transactions from the mempool, writing them all to a list, adding the header to form a block, and repeatedly guessing random numbers in the 'nonce' section of the header until the SHA256 hash of the header is of equal or lower value than the target threshold. The randomly guessed number is found in the part of the block labelled 'nonce', which just stands for: number only used once.

This (huge) number is the solution to the complicated maths problem SHA256, and, as you can probably infer, this number is only used once; the probability of two blocks having the same solution to the mining problem is practically zero.

It's worth noting exactly how this number is considered the solution: due to the impossibility of reverse-engineering the SHA256 maths problem to figure out what nonce would return a number below the target threshold, miners must simply guess from an immensely large set of possible solutions until they find a valid one. The kicker is that each time they guess a number, they have to calculate the hash again to see if it is correct, expending electricity with each computation. The nonce is just a space in the header reserved for making these guesses.

Naturally, the smaller the target threshold, the harder it is to hit. Thus, the target threshold determines the difficulty of mining. However, it's still a numbers game, so a greater difficulty means that miners will have to perform more hashes until they find a header with a hash below the threshold value.

The total amount of computing power dedicated to mining Bitcoin is measured by calculating the rate at which hashes are being attempted. Hence, it's called the 'hashrate' — whenever you hear hashrate, just think of it as the total amount of global effort miners are dedicating to mining new blocks.

As the total hashrate rate grows or shrinks, the mining difficulty increases or decreases accordingly, aiming at a directly proportional relationship between hashrate and difficulty. This mechanism ensures that miners always take approximately ten minutes to create new blocks, regardless of the network's hashrate. This system is called Proof of Work.

Curing the disease rather than aiding a symptom

Instead of catching thieves and then 'makin' 'em pay!' Bitcoin prefers to take its payment upfront; you have to *pay* to attempt theft. This is precisely what makes Bitcoin unique. Nakamoto saw that a peer-to-peer digital cash system would have already existed if it weren't for ever-present bad actors. He understood that the incentive to steal is almost always monetary gain. He realised that a digital democracy would grant malicious users disproportionate voting power ... so he designed a system whereby expending electricity grants governance and avoids autocracy, all while gifting good guys with transaction fees that prevent network congestion and block rewards (see 'Transactional data', page 71) that distribute new Bitcoins onto the market.

Additionally, the rewards cause competition and the resulting growth in computing power dedicated to securing the network makes being the good guy *more profitable* than being the bad guy ... which, as I'm sure you can imagine, IS A BIG F*CKING DEAL.

Lightning

The issue with organising a blockchain like this is speed and cost; having the block size this low effectively limits the maximum transactions per second of the chain, increasing transaction fees. However, there has been some brilliant work on solving this problem without sacrificing the elegance and decentralisation of small block sizes.

The 'Lightning Network' solution, proposed in 2015, is categorised as a 'layer-two solution' to the block-size/transactional-bandwidth problem. Since settling transactions on the public ledger requires a fee for miners, the Lightning Network allows users to set up peer-to-peer payment channels that can span large portions of the network, allowing people to trade written-and-signed transactions between each other *before* publicly broadcasting them to the ledger. This enables transactions to be settled instantly and much more cheaply because, at the end of a predetermined period, the resulting state of all transactions that occurred within a lightning payment channel is broadcast to the public ledger. Therefore, my mate Manni and I can buy a thousand coffees before we ever pay a single transaction fee to miners.

Think of it like setting up a bar tab. Rather than pay a transaction fee every time you order a drink, you keep tabs on who owes what and settle all transactions at the end of the night, only paying a transaction fee once.

The Lightning Network is a hugely innovative technology, and my explanation was simplified, so I strongly recommend learning more about it online if you feel inclined. YouTube is an excellent place to start; look at some learning materials by Andreas Antonopoulos for anything tech-related and go from there.

For a full explanation of the technology behind Bitcoin, I recommend Andreas's book *Mastering Bitcoin*. It remains the most comprehensive book on the technology of Bitcoin that I've ever read. In conclusion, you don't need to understand *everything* about Bitcoin. Don't obsess too much over how it works because every question you answer will lead to ten more questions.

It's just not a horizon worth chasing for most people. Unless you, too, are inclined to be somewhat of a horizon-chaser.

I once heard someone say, 'If you had invested £500 into Bitcoin in 2012, then today you would still have no idea how it works!' I think that's a good quote to end this chapter before it gets too long.

8
What are altcoins?

Phew! That last chapter was quite intense, but I couldn't live with myself if I wrote a book about Bitcoin without spending at least one chapter on the brilliance of the technology. However, I failed to mention one thing: the Bitcoin protocol is entirely open-source, meaning that anybody can view the source code. So, anyone who knows how to copy-and-paste can create another Bitcoin ... kind of.

One of the positive effects of this is, of course, the transparency. Bitcoin must be one of the most heavily peer-reviewed technological innovations in history due to the sheer number of people trying to hack it. It also means that should anyone succeed in the impossible task of destroying all Bitcoin nodes, some kid with a copy of the source code could restart the Bitcoin project in a weekend.

Still, there is another effect of Bitcoin being open-source — alternative coins. Ah, yes, the famed 'altcoins'. Oh boy ... it's a mess out there, but I'm going to do my best to explain.

DJ! Remix the track!

Bitcoin introduced blockchain technology, and it successfully
enabled decentralised permissionless consensus ... but it's
just a database of transactions. Humans use computers
for much more than just databases; we have games, apps,
exchanges, and other forms of intelligent software that
typically operate on centralised databases and servers.

That was until a man by the name of Vitalik Buterin
had the idea of building a blockchain capable of digital
transactions and running fully-fledged apps. So, he invented
an altcoin called Ethereum to do precisely that — well,
'precisely' might be a poor choice of words there — and
technically he's still doing it. Like, there were a couple of
complications along the way, but I mean, it's all part of
the process, right? These things just take time, okay?
It's complicated ... he just needs some space.

The great misconception of crypto

I will use Ethereum as a talking point since most altcoins are
called 'ERC-20' tokens, meaning they run on the Ethereum
network. Many other projects attempt to do what Ethereum
is doing, so it's a good example.

Ethereum is not a competitor to Bitcoin, just as a gold
watch isn't a competitor to gold. They are *entirely different
things*. Without starting too many wars, I'll begin by saying
Ethereum doesn't compete with Bitcoin on solving the
money problem, it doesn't even come close, and that's fine
because it *isn't* Bitcoin, and it's not trying to be either.

Altcoins and Bitcoin are entirely different things. I'm
emphasising this because I often hear, 'Bitcoin isn't scarce
because there are thousands of other cryptocurrencies

just like it.' This is incorrect. There is not a single cryptocurrency like Bitcoin, just as there isn't a single other metal with the molecular makeup of gold. However, the relationship between Bitcoin and altcoins is similar to that of gold and gold watches, since watches are complicated, modular, fragile, and have utility beyond their constituent parts. With that out of the way, let's talk about *why* this is the case.

It's like a computer, but, like, in the cloud ... you know?

So, the main component that sets Ethereum apart from Bitcoin is the introduction of the Ethereum Virtual Machine (EVM for short). The EVM is most easily conceptualised as a decentralised computer, to which anyone can lend their processing power for ether rewards, the cryptocurrency of Ethereum. When you use the internet, let's say YouTube, your computer sends messages to some warehouse stacked to the brim with internet-enabled computers that process your message and execute its instructions, such as 'search for cute cat videos'. The result of your request is then delivered back to you, the client. This server/client system makes it hard for anyone to provide their services or software without using a third-party company to ... well ... serve the service.

Global computer

Imagine you are Netflix, and you would like to serve your customers with high-quality movies and TV shows. Firstly, you will need somewhere to store those shows, and then you will need infrastructure to broadcast those shows across the globe. You will likely need to rent space on a server from whatever company owns it, and that company has the right to decline. But what if the server company owns 90 per cent of all servers worldwide and suddenly decides they don't like you? There's not much you can do about it except set up a personal server, but what if people were already running personal servers? The Ethereum Virtual Machine is the first network of computers, all acting as small servers, requiring no trust, all being rewarded for their service and without the need for any third party. Well… at least, that's the idea.

Not quite there yet

This sounds amazing, right? I mean, it seems to be the perfect way to decentralise the internet even more, and it all works perfectly! Well, that's where we run into some issues; it doesn't work as well as we would hope. Ethereum is the only altcoin project that has undergone significant pressure and use in the real world. Considering the tremendous ambition of the project, it's done impressively well. However, transaction fees are disastrously high, the network is still slow, and it is by no means anything near a finished project. Perhaps the biggest concern with the project is the intention for the underlying consensus mechanism of the entire Ethereum blockchain (currently called Proof of Work — similar to Bitcoin's Proof of Work algorithm described in the previous chapter) to be swapped out for an entirely different one called Proof of Stake (PoS). Proof of Stake distributes voting and block-validating power based on the monetary value someone locks up in escrow. This value acts as a sort of security deposit of truth, which the validator will not get back if they attempt to deceive the network. This means that governance and wealth have a much tighter relationship. Some say Proof of Stake risks turning Ethereum into a plutocracy, where the wealthy make all the decisions.

The blockchain trilemma

Another interesting thing to note about many of these altcoins (at the time of writing there are around 18,000 available) is that a large number of them aren't decentralised; they only plan to become decentralised at some point in the future, and they use this intention to declare themselves a decentralised project.

'There ain't no such thing as a free lunch' is a common economic phrase used to explain the basic idea that everything is a trade-off, and it aptly describes blockchain innovation. Many projects that have more functionalities will be more centralised, many that are faster will be less secure, many that are less centralised will be less scalable and so on. These problems that crypto projects are often making trade-offs between are often referred to as the 'blockchain trilemma', which includes:

1. **Scalability**
2. **Decentralisation**
3. **Security**

Almost all altcoins aim to solve this trilemma of problems in various ways; decentralisation and security seem to be the first to go in most cases. Those are the attributes of sound money and are Bitcoin's highest priority. This is funny, because many altcoin projects sacrifice those attributes, favouring speed and scalability, only to call themselves 'the next Bitcoin!' Therefore, no other projects compete with Bitcoin to solve the money problem. They're entirely different things.

NFTs

This combination of three letters took the world by storm in 2021, and it may be for good reason. NFT stands for non-fungible token. Does that mean anything to anyone? Probably not. First, we must define this idea of fungibility: what is fungibility and what makes something non-fungible?

For something to be fungible means that it is mutually interchangeable with another identical item. For instance, when you send your friend £10 from your bank account, you can't decide *which* £10 pounds to send. You have never considered this to be a problem because money is *fungible*: each penny in your account is the same as any other penny, and they're all mutually interchangeable. Bitcoin is also fungible; one Bitcoin is the same as any other. However, what if we created digital assets that were unique? What if we could create a Bitcoin that was uniquely identifiable? This is the idea of non-fungible tokens.

Now, I'm sure you are wondering why we would want to do this. Let's take an example: say you wanted to invent a way for Netflix subscriptions to be anonymous and tradable. If we could create a digital access card — like a digital version of a physical gym access card — that isn't tied to the identity of its possessor, then you could buy that access card from Netflix and sell it to your friend rather than cancelling your subscription. You wouldn't have to give Netflix your email address either. But wait, this sounds like a one-time purchase, but Netflix is a subscription service!

Well, this would be a problem in the physical realm of gym memberships, because to implement a monthly payment system the gym must associate your access card with your personal identity to charge monthly payments to your bank account, which is all dependent on a 'terms & conditions' contract you sign when you sign up for the subscription.

However, we are not playing in the physical realm. Because this card is digital, we can write code terms to it that, upon specified conditions, automatically streams funds from its owner to Netflix, regardless of who owns it. You can think of this code as a smart, automated version of Netflix's terms & conditions contract. The card in this example is an NFT, and the code is a smart contract. This is one example of how non-fungible tokens could be used in the future to open new avenues of trade and birth new economic frontiers, bypassing many of the inefficiencies of current digital infrastructure.

I'm sure you've also heard of the NFT digital art use case. Digital artists have existed for over two decades now and, for the most part, they are yet to find a way to monetise their work due to the struggles of owning — and therefore buying — digital art. NFTs could see the end of this struggle sometime in the near future by making unique digital tokens that represent ownership of digitally collectable art.

The main hurdle in the way of NFTs today is the fact that we are yet to see NFT technology become practical, decentralised or cheap. However, with some thought and innovation, I'm sure we will see Bitcoin-secured NFTs soon, and at that point we will see the birth of entirely new economies and industries in the sphere of digital assets.

So ... altcoins?

I explained the purpose of Ethereum because its intention to move from Proof of Work to Proof of Stake highlights the most important thing to understand about altcoins at this stage: *altcoins are experiments.* Ethereum has been signalling its intention to move towards a Proof of Stake-based system for a long time now; years in fact. At the time of writing, estimates are that it will transition sometime in 2022 (it may very well *not* happen, as they have been saying 'in a few months' for a few years now). At that point, every project built upon EVM will have to keep their ear to the ground and listen for any explosions ... metaphorically speaking.

The most important thing to take away from this chapter is that the altcoin world is attracting some brilliant people, which is hugely beneficial for advancing distributed-ledger tech, unless (and it's a big unless) altcoin mania causes the initial vision of blockchain to be obscured by corporate interests capitalising on the hype and advertising half-baked projects with buzzwords and calling it innovation. That's a very specific example because it's already happening. Before you throw your money at these work-in-progress coins, ask yourself one question: why does this project need a blockchain? If you can answer that, ask yourself why it requires a token or coin. Most of the time, the answer will be that it doesn't.

Regardless, looking past all the hype and altcoin mania, some exciting innovation is occurring in the blockchain space. The technology has the potential to impact industries other than banking. Still, banking and money are the foundation of *every* other industry, so don't underestimate the magnitude of the snowball effect that any improvements could bring.

Part three:
The future

9
You

It's looking like Bitcoin is here to stay. The capabilities and avenues that Bitcoin unlocks to move towards a less centralised world are enormous. So, this raises the question: what should you do about it?

Re-inventing the wheel

I think that re-inventing the wheel gets a bad rap. Wheels used to be terrible! The invention of precision ball-bearings used in the axles of wheels has dramatically increased the energy efficiency of the wheel by reducing friction, and although the basic *idea* for the wheel has remained the same forever, improvements can always be made. However, they aren't always needed.

The motor was another brilliant re-invention of the wheel, but that doesn't mean the rolling pin in your kitchen should run on petrol. I'm being a little tongue-in-cheek here, but I'm trying to say that not everything needs blockchain; some record-keeping is more aptly suited to centralised databases, specifically forms that don't deal with the allocation of value or valuables.

Blockchain is a technology designed to protect against the threat of human incentives to act selfishly by lying or stealing (a.k.a. altering the true chain of ownership of goods). If you have a database of all your bird-watching findings, I doubt you need to place that database on a decentralised data-storage solution like blockchain; you'd have to be one paranoid birdwatcher to do that. There may be some use cases if you are a business owner, especially if you own a huge business. However, they aren't quite industry-ready at the time of writing.

Let's get vulnerable

No, not in a therapy-session kind of way (I'll save that for another book), but we are all vulnerable little creatures. Firstly, although we only require the same energy as a light bulb, our bodies are a little more stubborn than light bulbs when it comes to the conditions under which they will turn on. Maybe most notable among them is that we have a very narrow temperature range within which we will survive; if your body temperature reaches roughly above 42°c or below 15°c, it will turn off permanently. Luckily, we can buy houses and food to avoid this. Hence, food and shelter are layer-one energy because they accommodate our existence. However, that's where another bag of vulnerabilities comes in: the layer-two energy we use to acquire those goods, a.k.a. money.

Money is the most prominent point of vulnerability to which blockchain offers protection.

Self-defence

With most central banks around the world printing money,
thus diluting its purchasing power, your monetary energy,
supposedly represented by your bank balance, leaves
your possession without your consent. The agreement to
trade your energy or value for its monetary equivalent was
broken at the whim of a decision-maker who isn't you or
your employer. So, at the risk of sounding like a nutcase,
your savings are being stolen from you by the government
to bail themselves out of spending deficits caused by their
mismanagement of your tax money.

Essentially, the government can be thought of as a
friend suffering from addiction. Unfortunately, they have
found themselves in a sticky situation and are relying
on you to help them get through it — but would you be
helping them by funding their habit?

(Currently) the best thing you can do

These government-created currencies are called 'fiat money'
which roughly translates from Latin to 'it shall be money'.
This is because these currencies are only money because
the government has declared them as such by force.
Suppose you continue to store your wealth in fiat currency.
In that case, you are *allowing* bad monetary policy to
continue to eat away your purchasing power, acting as an
enabler to your nation's addiction to the money printer.

These days, you vote with your money much more than
with the lesser-of-two-evils decision you make during
the national popularity contest of your given nation.
Therefore, by holding your savings in a fiat currency
(money declared by a government to be legal tender),

you vote for the fiat system. By allowing the redistribution of your purchasing power from you to the financial sector, you're unknowingly a *benefactor* to wealth inequality. Just as an addict will trick you into funding their addiction, the government has tricked you into subsidising theirs by diluting your monetary energy rather than taking the monetary batteries you store it in.

It's just watering down the liquor all over again, but with extra steps and fancier terminology. Although, when things get *really* bad, governments probably won't give you the courtesy of hiding it from you. Remember when the United States government took all their own citizens' gold with Executive Order 6102? (Or search 'Cyprus bail-in' for another example).

So, you're hopeless, right? Not quite ... Bitcoin is the first decentralised monetary network *engineered* as such. A riverbank for those to whom the tide isn't kind. I will admit, the payments infrastructure for Bitcoin isn't brilliant in its current form, and so you will likely need to own a certain amount of fiat money to pay for everyday expenses, depending on where you live.

However, your monetary energy, which you don't intend to spend, is much safer stored in Bitcoin. Unlike fiat, Bitcoin is a battery that no single entity can decide to drain for their benefit whenever they choose.

At the time of writing, Bitcoin has seen a major drop in value due to its four-year 'boom and bust' cycle. However, the market has shown a constant and non-negligible demand for Bitcoin. The most significant risk in buying Bitcoin is probably losing your password. Yes, the price and value can fluctuate (of course, there is turbulence when you're on a rocket ship), but would you prefer to risk temporarily losing a chunk of purchasing power quickly?

Or would you rather slowly but surely lose it all? If you own a business, the same question applies to your company's savings and balance sheet. Using Bitcoin to store your monetary energy is the best way that anyone can get involved, and you can do it today.

It's a tie...

The list of 'Best ways to get involved in blockchain' has a joint first place, between using Bitcoin as a store of value and accepting Bitcoin as payment for your product/service.

Whether you are an employee or a business owner, you can always mention that you accept Bitcoin as payment. One of the most common ways to accept Bitcoin payments is with invoicing and conversion services for sellers, reducing the friction of fiddly Bitcoin payments. However, many of these services convert the Bitcoin you receive into your local currency and pay it directly to your bank ... essentially, they just sell the Bitcoin you receive. There's nothing inherently wrong with this approach (sorry to the Bitcoiners who will hate me for saying that), but if you want to offer Bitcoin payment optionality for your customers without feeling exposed to the natural price fluctuations of Bitcoin, then sure, go for it, so long as you are aware that you are trading the risk of *potentially* losing cash, for the risk of *definitely* losing money via inflation.

When choosing the lesser of two evils, we humans tend to overestimate the risks of action and underestimate the risks of inaction. The best way for you to accept Bitcoin is with a service that allows you to receive it to a wallet owned by you or your company and leave it alone as if it were in a bank. I won't name any companies or infrastructure for doing this, but with a quick Google search and half an hour of research, you should have a good idea of how to acquire Bitcoin. Just ensure that you are only using legitimate and established software and hardware to buy and store your Bitcoin; there's no need to stray from the trodden path in that regard.

10
Room for good

I have talked a lot about blockchain's capacity to revolutionise multiple industries in the future. Yet, in the previous chapter, when discussing what you can do to get involved, I haven't provided any examples beyond Bitcoin. This chapter will explain why.

But what about all those other uses of blockchain?

The average person doesn't need to worry about the various use cases of distributed-ledger technology. This is for a few reasons:

1. The infrastructure is yet to be laid.

2. The durability of many blockchains is yet to be tested by time.

3. Until the blockchain industry is met by more innovation, the costs often outweigh the benefits for most uses of distributed databases in small-to-medium businesses.

Essentially, it's just so freakin' early. Just as the uses of the internet were yet to be discovered thirteen years into its lifespan (circa 1996), it's safe to assume that blockchain today, thirteen years into its lifespan (actually, it's the thirteenth birthday of Bitcoin as I write), is yet to define the various forms it will embody in the future. However, the core invention of the internet, the ability to send information long distances instantly, which revolutionised the postal service, is still serving that purpose today.

Similarly, the core invention of the blockchain, the ability to send money long distances instantly, revolutionising the banking industry, will likely still serve that purpose years from now. So, keep an eye on the blockchain industry, don't let it sweep you under the rug, be aware that someday soon you may have to adapt your business to the market as the market is adapting to blockchain, but don't be a 'dot-com-boom' guy or gal either. Those who were overly evangelical in the early days of the internet invested in any 'internet company' that could be bothered to do an IPO (initial public offering of shares). These days, they're called 'crypto guys', and they invest in any and every blockchain project that can be bothered to do an ICO (initial coin offering).

The truth is that most cryptocurrencies will fail because they don't need to be cryptocurrencies, and most blockchain projects will fail because they don't need blockchains.

The electricityphant in the room ...

I almost feel wrong for getting this far into the book without mentioning the most prominent criticism of Bitcoin and blockchain: the use of electricity. I'm sure you've heard it before: 'Bitcoin uses more energy than entire countries!'

Yeah, well, so do Christmas lights in America, so ... it's easy to make a headline sound like a thesis if you cherry-pick your point of reference.

This isn't me discrediting the argument, however. Any rational person should be worried when they hear of something using lots of energy. However, the energy argument doesn't quite stand up after a little bit of digging ... quite literally. Digging for oil has been one of the most lucrative businesses in human history due to our dependence on energy to survive and advance; all human progress is directly linked to our improvements in extracting, manipulating and concentrating energy towards our latest concept of utopia. So as a relatively primitive species, we have fought a hell of a lot over our toys. A member of the United States Space Force and avid Bitcoin advocate, Jason P. Lowery, spends much time talking about the use of energy in Bitcoin. He gives due thought to Bitcoin's energy use and the energy consumption of *not* using Bitcoin.

Remember when I said, 'We humans tend to overestimate the dangers of action and underestimate the risks of inaction'? To have an honest conversation regarding the costs of Bitcoin's energy consumption, we must also discuss the costs of the alternative. In fact, not only do I believe this to be one of the most critical topics in Bitcoin, but I believe that its importance lies in emphasising Bitcoin's potential to be part of the *solution* to emissions, rather than a problem. Stick with me here, it's about to get weird again.

Yet again, I am asking for your imagination's support

Let's imagine Planet Earth as a petri dish, where the various species of mammals that inhabit the land are the bacteria within. For want of a better word, bacteria's 'goal' is to duplicate and propagate their genetic signature through time; the goal of a tree is to plant its seeds. On the part of the individual cell, its responsibility is to grow large enough to divide itself into two parts and ensure that each half is equipped to do the same thing. In this scenario, the individual cells are mammals (yes, that includes you, ya dirty animal), so they differ from cells in one primary way: cells are asexually reproductive, whereas mammals are sexually reproductive. This means it takes two mammals to make an offspring, rather than each being capable of reproducing independently.

Re-defining violence

This means that humans now have a choice to make: with whom do I want my child to share my genes? This little idiosyncrasy turns out to be the primary driving factor of human behaviour and transforms our little petri-dish experiment into a breeding ground for sexual advertisement. Choosing a mate isn't a minor decision, either, as it could be the difference between your child surviving or dying. Unfortunately, it's not so easy to pick and choose your partner. This is especially true if you don't have many options to choose from … and so begins the undying scramble towards sexual desirability.

A large part of that equation is power. In the case of most mammals, the females want males who can protect them and their children, since having a child is inherently riskier and requires more investment from the female. The males are very aware of this, so an eternal competition for power ensues. This often becomes violent and bloody, which is okay (as far as Mother Nature is concerned) until the violence becomes so rampant that it threatens the survival of the entire species and is counter-productive to the production of children.

So, evolution has slowly but surely discovered ways to regulate this violence. Intelligent lifeforms need to find out who the top dog is, to form the social hierarchies required to ensure that the arbiter of resource allocation isn't always physical violence. In other words, it's better to have one fight and remember who won than to fight every time you smell food, and it's even better still to know who would win the fight beforehand and never bother playing it out on the board.

We're just trying not to go extinct, man

Violence accelerates natural selection, but if nature is too selective, eventually there will be nothing left to select from; the species will go extinct. So, what happens instead? You begin to see animals such as moose, deer, rhinoceros and various insects growing 'proof of strength' out of their skulls in magnificent antlers and horns or vibrant colours. This allows the strongest to prove their dominance simply with a show of their antlers rather than a violent fight. If you thought humans don't do this, you'd be wrong.

You could argue that nuclear weaponry is a prime modern example of this: our best effort to protect our land and wealth from each other without decimating the gene pool is by creating nuclear weapons. It's a situation of mutually assured destruction. Picture the world's nations standing on opposite ends of a seesaw hovering above a 5,000ft drop while aiming atom bombs at each other — each could annihilate the other. Still, it would assure their own destruction in the process. Yes, our species' survival depends on us not falling out with each other.

Until recent times, all wealth was physical, so the protection of that wealth was military and looked ... I could say it looked 'equally physical' but, let's be honest, it looked like lone mothers and empty coffins. History doesn't get any prettier the longer you look, and there's no reason to believe that the future will read differently unless we change the way we determine who the top dog is. Violence was all well and good when we were tribes of ten, but now we are nations of a billion, armed to march ourselves into extinction and equipped with enough nuclear weaponry to bring thousands of other species with us.

This notion of mutually assured destruction is bittersweet. On the one hand, we could end our species, and on the other hand, we probably won't because that sucks for everyone. Yet the main issue I have with this protection system is that it is prevention through promised retaliation — but you can't 'un-bomb' Pearl Harbor by nuking Hiroshima. This is where Bitcoin comes into play again (bear with me).

We can learn a lot from Bitcoin's defence system. Rather than implementing some governmental body on the network to punish people who break the rules, the Bitcoin network is built in a way that disincentivises dishonesty in the first place. Because it's so expensive even to attempt to gain a sufficient share of the Bitcoin network's mining power to rewrite the chain in your favour, your unlikely success would be nullified by your expensive means of achieving it.

It's like mutually assured destruction in that both systems disincentivise offence while incentivising defence, except that should an attempt be made to 'invade' the Bitcoin network, all that'd be lost would be time, money and energy, rather than the countless lives, livelihoods and environmental progress lost during the invasion of a nation.

War is proof of work

One presupposition some people infer from this argument is that Bitcoin will somehow end wars, which I do not believe to be true. The argument states that wealth stored in physical goods must be protected by physical force, or, as Jason P. Lowery says, 'kinetic energy'. In contrast, wealth held in Bitcoin is protected by electrical energy. But money isn't the only form of wealth. Other things such as land and materials may still be incentives for invasion by 'the guy with the bigger stick'. However, they wouldn't get a big pot of gold in a central bank vault for their troubles if they did.

Bitcoin mining attempts to replicate the sacrifice of energy required to mine gold — except instead of oil, explosives, machinery and workers, it's electricity that's sacrificed instead. Previously, when gold was money, its value was backed by its *scarcity*. Subsequently, the Bretton Woods system backed US dollars with gold. However, after the abolition of Bretton Woods in 1971, the US dollar became volatile and lost value. The United States government needed something else to back the currency, so they struck a deal with Saudi Arabia, agreeing that all oil sold by Saudi Arabia was to be priced in US dollars; the rest of the oil-exporting countries soon followed suit. This meant that anyone who wanted to buy oil from these major exporters would have to buy dollars to pay for the oil.

This ensured a constant demand for US dollars and is one of the primary reasons the US dollar is still the world's reserve currency. However, remember those pesky incentives? Well, oil is infamously bad for the environment, and now its production tightens the United States' grip on global commerce. It's almost as if the world's most powerful country is actively disincentivised from investing in the development of green-energy production technology.

If only a monetary network could act as an ever-present customer for cheap, clean energy. Under such circumstances, the powers that be might actually invest in the development of said systems … oh, wait.

In conclusion

I began studying Bitcoin to decide if it was a good investment or not. As I studied, the spotlight strayed from my financial concerns. Instead, it was drawn to the world. The world is in a great place right now; I won't make the claim that we live during a historical tragedy. However, from excessive waste to poverty and oppression, there's much work still to be done. The problems facing the world today are beyond the individual. Fixing them is outside the reach of any politician or political ideology. It would require the very fabric of cooperation to change.

Money is the very fabric of cooperation.

Bitcoin changed it.

FAQ

Here are some of the most-asked questions about Bitcoin/ cryptocurrency and their short-form answers, with references back to the relevant page number where the topic is discussed in more detail.

Will the government ban crypto?

Some governments may ban some cryptocurrency projects. Depending on how centralised a project is, a governmental ban may indeed cause some projects to fail. (However, Bitcoin, which has unparalleled decentralisation, is immune to the threat of government bans.) There are many governments, but there is one Bitcoin network; if any single government bans Bitcoin, it presents an opportunity for another country to benefit from the fast-growing industry. China banned Bitcoin mining in 2021, and the rest of the world's Bitcoin mining efforts became more lucrative. For more on why Bitcoin is immune to bans, see Chapter 7.

Who invented Bitcoin?

We don't know who invented Bitcoin. Therefore, we don't know who invented blockchain either. It was an anonymous individual (or potentially a group) claiming to be a Japanese man by the name of Satoshi Nakamoto, and they did an excellent job of hiding their identity. This was likely an intentional choice to protect Satoshi from potential adversaries and protect the Bitcoin network from developing a centralised leadership structure. See pages 64–65.

What if I lose my Bitcoin?

If you lose the password to your Bitcoin, there's no 'reset password' option; you — and only you — are responsible for keeping your coins safe. That's what makes them *your* coins. If there were an email that you could send to a tech-support group to retrieve your lost coins, that would make the tech-support group a centralised point of control. This would (counter-intuitively) make Bitcoin easier to lose since that centralised point of control could be hacked, and you could have your Bitcoin stolen through no fault of your own. See Chapter 7.

What is blockchain?

Blockchain is a form of record-keeping technology that allows for the decentralised maintenance of a shared ledger. There are many forms of blockchain, but the original blockchain was created by Satoshi Nakamoto in 2009. See page 72.

Can Bitcoin be hacked?

The short answer: no. The long answer: noooooooooo. Okay, I'm kidding, the reason Bitcoin can't be hacked is not quickly explainable, so I will give you a simile and a page number: Attempting to hack Bitcoin for monetary gain is like paying £1,000 for a gun so that you can steal a packet of crisps worth 50p. See pages 73–75.

About the author

Angelo Morgan-Somers is a young Bitcoin analyst and consultant from Wales. When he was 12 years old, he sustained a severe injury to the spleen during a parkour competition and was told by doctors that he might have to confront his mortality in the coming weeks. This front-row seat to the scarcity of time caused him to drop out of school later that year to educate himself online, hoping he could do so in a faster and more efficient way. One year later, he discovered Bitcoin and began his journey down the rabbit hole of learning. He spent the ensuing years familiarising himself with the world of cryptocurrency and helped grow multiple seven-figure cryptocurrency portfolios and advised security practices through his consultancy services. However, all roads eventually lead back to Bitcoin.

Now, he is aiming to help onboard a new generation of people to Bitcoin by questioning the axioms of our monetary paradigm.

Thanks

Firstly, I'd like to thank my big brother and partner-in-crime, Theo, for teaching me the meaning of work ethic, discipline and perseverance. You set the bar that I try to reach.

My dad, for introducing me to Bitcoin, thereby catalysing my journey. And for the magnitude of everything else of which you were — and are — an unknowing catalyst.

My mum, for keeping my chin up, and being a walking reminder that the cliché 'diamonds are made under pressure' really is true.

And Satoshi Nakamoto, for providing the antidote to pessimism.

Index

Books in the series

Also available

Available in print, digital and audio formats from booksellers or via our website: **thedobook.co**

To hear about events, forthcoming titles and our book club, find us on social media **@dobookco**, or subscribe to our newsletter